W9-ATN-292

Being Enough

*A book
of inspirational reflections.
by:*

LEIGH SANDERS

FAIR'S ARBOR PRESS
NEWNAN, GEORGIA

All rights reserved. Printed in the United States of America.
No part of this book may be used or reproduced in any manner
whatsoever without written permission of the publisher.

For ordering information please contact:
Fair's Arbor Press
684 Jim Starr Road
Newnan, Georgia 30263
(404) 521-2703

Cover Design / Book Design by Yellowhouse, Inc.

All Photography by Leigh Sanders

Copyright 1997 by Leigh Sanders
Fair's Arbor Press, Newnan, Georgia

Printed January, 1997 by The Stinehour Press, Lunenburg, Vermont
with permission of the copyright owner

ISBN: 0-9656435-0-6

Library of Congress Card Number: 97-90009

Table of Contents

Volume One

Introduction

Change comes to all of us. Interruptions in our worldly plans, obstacles to our ambitions. And failures come. Failures in our relationships and in our expectations of outer world success. All of these are the phenomena of change, self-conflict and self-doubt.

Six or seven years ago I encountered all of these challenges. These difficult conditions quickly tested my notion of who I really was.

This time required, no, demanded that I examine how I defined myself, what I believed about God, about me, and about life and death. And this time required that I decide how I would choose to live and die.

I looked for help in all the places our culture expects to find it in times like this - psychiatry, astrology, meditation, religious teachings, yoga and books, lots of books. Books of all the current thinking on holistic self-concepts, self-analysis and awareness.

For years I dutifully explored the dark side of my person, which was that part of me most often present. Gratefully, I found no analytical contradictions, regardless the approach to self. It increasingly seemed to me that truth rested at the center of all life and all paths to enlightenment led, like spokes in a cosmic wheel, to that truth.

Then, on a trip to see yet another of God's way-showers, I revisited the mountains of Western North Carolina, the towns of Murphy, Hayesville, Franklin, Bryson City, Fontana, Robbinsville and Andrews. And I visited the wonderful reaches of the Nantahala National Forest with its hundreds of miles of gravel roads that wind deep into the heart of that mountain range.

As I rode for days on end in my truck, I began to feel in the natural surroundings a sense of assurance, a oneness with the natural world that became to me an affirmation of the worthiness of life, all life, my life. It was then, for the very first time in 1994, that I began to write down what I was hearing and feeling and to take pictures of the scenes that inspired these thoughts. I hiked, I camped, sat on remote mountain tops, explored whole mountain ranges off any beaten trail. I couldn't get close enough to all this natural abundance. The result was a continuous confirmation of the simple beauty of life without everyday struggle and without annual agendas.

I have written down these thoughts for me. As soon as I would decide that my reflections pertained to a past difficulty, I would encounter a life passage to which the piece was even more appropriate. A lifetime friend observed that I was getting the answers before God gave me the test. And I am so grateful for that.

I share the first of these books with you in the faith that these reflections will connect you with that part of you that holds your strength and unconditional compassion for yourself, the seat of your self-love and irrevocable self-approval. And I know that person you so want to be will surely meet you somewhere along this wonderful path.

Leigh Sanders

The River Waits

Effortlessly the stream

cascades down the face of the mountain.

Willingly moving aside as it passes the giant boulders that sit obstinately in its path.

Patiently it waits in pools

as the terrain levels in the stream's path, not wishing to move any more quickly

than is natural.

Content just to be in this one place,

grateful for the experience.

Trusting, as it waits, that the next passage will unfold as it should.

Knowing only that the river waits below,

that the destination is assured.

And no moment is scarred with the fear

that the stream's path is somehow unsafe ahead.

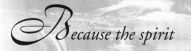 *Because the spirit*

that is the stream is constant, continuous and worthy of the trust it enjoys.

Would that we could live like this?

Effortlessly meeting the new day,

as our life sometimes cascades ahead of us in bursts of changing circumstance.

Willingly confronting the obstacles in our lives

and avoiding the temptation to paint them as problems.

Choosing rather to savor the rush of spontaneity they can introduce in our experience

of this particular time.

Patiently abiding the periods in our life passage during which activity wanes, visible progress

ceases and we have only to wait for our good to appear without struggle.

Content to be in this moment,

blessing the process and accepting the past with quiet gratitude.

Always trusting that the unknown, the unseen territory in our lives ahead

will manifest in a manner that will support us,

nurture us,

expand our spirit and allow us the room to grow.

Knowing only that, in the current of universal energy in which we bathe and flow,

the destination is assured. The peace we deserve and the love we seek will come to us,

when it will, as it will, as abundantly as we dreamed.

For we are safe

within the spirit of this life stream.

It is continuous, constant and worthy of our faith.

Too often forgetting this, we try too hard to control the flow and change the course.

And we trust too little that life will unfold for us in a way that will reward our faith with

wholeness

and completion.

But in the silence and serenity

of the pools in our lives,

we can know that always, always the river waits below.

And then we can feel

from the depths of our being

that our destination in peace is assured.

In the Quiet - an Assurance

Be still now

and listen to the silence.

Winter comes

and with it

the day's light isn't with us for long.

The trees,

barren against the brown of the mountain's cover,

don't speak now.

The streams even seem muffled,

less exuberant in their trek down the mountain.

Dry leaves rustling

with the sound of deer foraging, but very quietly.

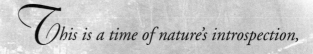

This is a time of nature's introspection,

of going within

and conserving strength.

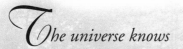

The universe knows

how to use this time and so should we.

We must trust that in these times

when our brilliance fades and our colors dim, that internally,

great work is taking place,

beyond our perception,

out beyond our consciousness.

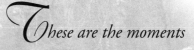

These are the moments

on which our future growth depends.

The strength we will express,

the personal power in our future life will begin here in the quiet.

So be still now.

Trust.

Feel the grace of this time and know

that you are growing - even now.

Times of Gray

Gray clouds promising snow.

Gray winds that drive the winter's cold swiftly down the valley.

Brown grass lying close to the ground in the long pasture,

as ice begins to cover the stream along the mountain road.

Gray days happen in winter,

Shutting out the sun.

Closing us off from the warmth and the light,

driving us to shelter.

Yet occasionally,

even during times like this, the clouds break.

Then the sun's brilliance explodes into our view, creating a wondrous bouquet

of every tree in the great hardwoods on the mountain.

Painting a shimmering silver image that captures every limb for just a moment.

Where seconds before

everything was dull and gray,

now there is brilliant definition in wonderful sparkling detail.

And we are amazed as we realize it was there all the time.

Spiritual enlightenment happens much the same way in our lives.

It comes to us only after long periods of difficulty

that seem to chill our sensitivity to everything.

Times that drive us away from our concept of who we are

and deny us our being.

Yet when truth does come to us,

it suddenly paints our life with meaning.

Illuminating the complexity in our experience,

bringing understanding where before there was only gray confusion.

And we endure the harshness of our emotional winters by holding

to the images uncovered by those divine bursts of awareness. We survive with the warmth of that

meaning captured in our soul space, sheltering us from the cold confusion blowing down the

valleys of our lives.

And, sitting with our backs to the cold harsh wind of our experience,

we hold to that memory knowing the meaning,

the purpose in our life, is there all the time.

Just waiting for us to awaken to our own capacity to comprehend and to find enduring peace

in that sacred understanding.

Being Enough

In its normal, undisturbed state,
nature is always enough.

There is always enough sunlight.
There are always enough trees in the forest.
There are always enough mountains to shelter the valleys.
There is always enough natural food for the animals and enough water in the streams.
And the eagle always flies high enough on wings that are always strong enough.

And in all this glorious natural world, nothing more is required for the mountains,
forest, and all that abide there, to be all God intended.

They are enough.

But as we,

in the hurry and struggle of our lives,

put ever greater distances between ourselves and our true nature,

we tend to forget that we too are enough.

In our striving to prove ourselves, to compete, to please, to succeed, we lose touch with our own

adequacy and our natural wholeness.

And why?

Most often because we are attempting to live a truth that is not ours,

to follow a path that is not natural for us.

We bend, stretch and reach beyond our grasp to achieve, to perform.

But for whom?

And then,

there are those among us,

men and women we encounter, who are being enough.

The writer who finds the words without struggle.

The composer musician for whom the melody is everlasting.

The teacher who conveys the message with such ease and thoroughness.

And we say of them,

"they were meant to do that, it comes to them so naturally."

Yes. Because they are living in the center of their truth.

And so can each of us live at the epicenter of our truth.

But how?

First, by accepting what we are not.

We are not defined by the measure of our material, professional success and achievement:
we are bigger than that.
We are not forever obligated to careers outside our truth:
we are broader than that.
We are not required to wager our personhood in an attempt to please anyone:
we are more precious than that.

So listen in faith within to hear the song
that is uniquely you.

And remember as you do, there are enough trees,
not one too many.

Whatever your gift,
your task, it is precisely what is needed.

Here? Yes, here. Now? Right now.

Listen to your song and move your life to its tempo.
That is the melody that only you can sing and that all the world wants to hear.

Because you too are enough.
Enough to fill the universal space reserved especially for your spirit.
Accept it, own it and leave the other tunes to someone else.

For like all the rest of nature, as you are about being, being enough - you will discover that
nothing more is required of you to be just as perfect as God intended.

There is great freedom in that.

For you were born to that energy.

Your life, from the very first moment, was tuned to that melody.

Your intuition knows every note.

Your spirit feels its compelling tempo.

Flow with it like the rushing stream.

Soar with it on eagle's wings.

Listen to your song and join the dance.

Live in the center of your truth and find the bliss of always

being enough.

The Greenness

Lush, Moist, Fresh.

The greenness of Spring arrives on the mountain

in urgent waves of foliage,

expanding daily to cover more of the bare structure that was there before,

completing the mountain's profile in rushes of green,

every imaginable shade of green.

This is the green of new growth.

The tenderness, the subtlety of Spring, silently arriving in fresh crisp sunlit mornings,

anointed with the soft scent

of all the wild flowering,

adorned with blossoms drenched in dew.

Look carefully in the early light.

This is your awakening.

This is your Spring.

This is the unfolding of your growth after a season of quiet spent patiently.

Here is the expression of your new strength,

your power to manifest the wonder of your unique spirit.

$\mathcal{Y}$ou have stored your energy for a time.

Now you find the expression of your person in fresh, new activity.

And every morning now, your new announcement of life fills you, asserting your wholeness,

the essence of your being.

This is the beginning.

A season to enjoy the natural abundance of all that you are becoming,

all that you deserve.

And these are the first signs of the wonderful promise that your future holds,

as you complete the spiritual structure your struggle has carved for your life.

And God smiles

as you experience the grand rebirth of your spirit,

the greenness of your personal Spring.